W9-ANG-408

Working with Others

by Robin Nelson

Series consultants: Sonja Green, MD, and
Distinguished Professor Emerita Ann Nolte, PhD,
Department of Health Sciences, Illinois State University

Lerner Publications Company • Minneapolis

Lerner Publications Company
A division of Lerner Publishing Group
241 First Avenue North
Minneapolis, MN 55401 U.S.A.

Website address: www.lernerbooks.com

Words in **bold type** are explained in a glossary on page 31.

Library of Congress Cataloging-in-Publication Data

Nelson, Robin, 1971–
    Working with others / by Robin Nelson.
      p.   cm. – (Pull ahead books)
    Includes index.
    ISBN-13: 978-0-8225-3486-0 (lib. bdg. : alk. paper)
    ISBN-10: 0-8225-3486-X (lib. bdg. : alk. paper)
    1. Interpersonal conflict–Juvenile literature. 2. Conflict
resolution–Juvenile literature. I. Title. II. Series.
    BF637.I48N45 2006
    303.6'9–dc22   2005017968

Manufactured in the United States of America
1 2 3 4 5 6 – JR – 11 10 09 08 07 06

You work and play with other people every day. Most of the time, you get along well. But sometimes people do or say things that you don't like.

Maybe
someone
takes one
of your toys.

Maybe you are blamed for something you didn't do.

Maybe someone calls you a mean name. Maybe you feel left out.

Maybe you argue with a friend. These things can make you angry.

It is okay to
feel angry
sometimes.
It is okay
to have
conflicts
with people.

What do people do when conflicts make them angry?

Some people yell and scream when they feel angry. Some people even hit other people.

Yelling, screaming, and hitting do not **solve** conflicts. They hurt people and make problems worse.

Some people walk away from conflicts.

They want to be alone when they feel angry. They need time to calm down.

Walking away is okay at first. But it won't solve anything. People need to work things out with each other.

People should talk about their feelings. Talking can solve conflicts. Talking can make everyone feel better.

We can solve conflicts without arguing. Take turns talking. Let everyone share his or her **opinion.**

Sometimes you will not agree with a person's opinion. Listen to what the other person is saying. Ask questions.

Use **respectful** words. Don't call each other names.

Apologize when you are wrong.

Make sure everyone has a chance to
speak. Then you can solve conflicts
together.

Think of ideas to solve the conflicts.
Decide which ideas will work best.

If you are stuck, ask an adult to help
you solve the conflicts.

Ask someone to help who will listen
and not take sides.

You might have to **compromise.**

Compromise means both sides must give up something to solve conflicts.

Solving conflicts peacefully takes
practice.

Work together! Solve conflicts as a team. Talk them out, and everyone will be happy!

Dealing with Anger

What do you do when you feel angry? You might feel too angry to talk about how you feel. Here are some ways for you to calm down and get the anger out.

■ Take deep breaths and count slowly.

■ Write down what happened and how you feel about it.

■ Draw a picture.

■ Listen to calm music.

■ Read a book.

■ Take a walk or do some other kind of exercise.

■ Pound on a pillow.

■ Stomp your feet.

Talking Things Out

When you feel a little better, it is time to talk. Here are some things to remember when talking things out.

■ Tell the other person how you feel and why you feel that way. Be honest.

■ Ask that person how he or she feels.

■ Remember that your body also tells a person how you are feeling. Show that you care about what he or she is saying. Don't cross your arms or make faces.

■ Look at the person you are speaking to. Do the same thing when the other person is speaking to you.

■ Listen carefully to what the other person has to say.

■ Wait for your turn to speak.

■ Apologize when you are wrong or if you hurt someone's feelings.

■ Try to find a way to do things differently next time.

Books and Websites

Aaron, Jane. *When I'm Angry.* New York: Golden Books, 1998.

Bang, Molly. *When Sophie Gets Angry—Really, Really Angry . . .* New York: Blue Sky Press, 1999.

Brown, Laurie Krasny, and Marc Brown. *How to Be a Friend: A Guide to Making Friends and Keeping Them.* Boston: Little, Brown, 1998.

Crary, Elizabeth. *I Want It.* Seattle: Parenting Press, 1996.

Polland, Barbara K. *We Can Work It Out: Conflict Resolution for Children.* Berkeley: Tricycle Press, 2000.

Scholes, Katherine. *Peace Begins with You.* San Francisco: Sierra Club Books, 1990.

Thomas, Pat. *Is It Right to Fight?: A First Look at Anger.* Hauppauge, NY: Barron's Educational Series, 2003.

Websites

Get Your Angries Out
http://www.angriesout.com/

KidsHealth
http://kidshealth.org/kid/

Out On a Limb: A Guide to Getting Along
http://www.urbanext.uiuc.edu/conflict/

Glossary

apologize: to say you are sorry about something

compromise: to solve a conflict by agreeing to accept something that is not exactly what you wanted

conflicts: fights or arguments

opinion: an idea, thought, or belief

respectful: polite or kind. Showing concern for other people's feelings.

solve: to find the answer to something

Index

Photo Acknowledgments

The photographs in this book appear courtesy of: © Todd Strand/Independent Picture Service, cover, pp. 15, 19, 28; © Stockbyte/SuperStock, pp. 3, 6; © Ariel Skelley/CORBIS, p. 4; © Richard Hutchings/CORBIS, p. 5; © Dex Images/CORBIS, p. 7; © age fotostock/SuperStock, pp. 8, 17, 21; © Norbert Schaefer/CORBIS, pp. 9, 25; © Grace/zefa/CORBIS, p. 10; © Susan Johns/Photo Researchers, Inc., p. 11; © H. Benser/zefa/CORBIS, p. 12; © Jose Luis Pelaez, Inc./CORBIS, p. 13; © Royalty-Free/CORBIS, pp. 14, 24; © Tom Stewart/CORBIS, p. 16; © Jiang Jin/SuperStock, p. 18; © Michael Keller/CORBIS, p. 20; © Gideon Mendel/CORBIS, p. 22; © Ed Bock/CORBIS, p. 23; © Randy Faris/CORBIS, p. 26; PhotoDisc Royalty Free by Getty Images, p. 27.